The Federal Reserve Board

A Consumer's Guide to
Mortgage
Refinancings

Table of contents

Have interest rates fallen? Or do you expect them to go up? Has your credit score improved enough so that you might be eligible for a lower-rate mortgage? Would you like to switch into a different type of mortgage?

The answers to these questions will influence your decision to refinance your mortgage. But before deciding, you need to understand all that refinancing involves. Your home may be your most valuable financial asset, so you want to be careful when choosing a lender or broker and specific mortgage terms. Remember that, along with the potential benefits to refinancing, there are also costs.

When you refinance, you pay off your existing mortgage and create a new one. You may even decide to combine both a primary mortgage and a second mortgage into a new loan. Refinancing may remind you of what you went through in obtaining your original mortgage, since you may encounter many of the same procedures—and the same types of costs—the second time around.

Mortgage shopping worksheet
—a dozen key questions to ask

	Current lender	Lender 1	Lender 2	Lender 3
What type of mortgage is it—fixed-rate, adjustable-rate, FHA, VA, other?				
What is the loan term (length of loan)?				
What is the contract interest rate or starting interest rate?				
Can the balance you owe on the loan rise?				
Does the loan payment include an escrow or reserve for taxes and insurance?				
What is the estimated total monthly payment (principal, interest, taxes, insurance, PMI)?				
What are the estimated fees and other settlement (closing) costs?				
Does this loan have a prepayment penalty? If so, how much could it be?				
Does this loan have a balloon payment? If so, how much is it?				
If the loan has an adjustable rate*:				
When is the first rate adjustment?				
What is the most the rate could be at the first rate adjustment?				
What is the most the monthly payments (for principal and interest) could be after the first rate adjustment *and* over the life of the loan?				

Based on the answers to these questions, and after calculating your break-even period, you may want to get more detailed information. You can use our *In-Depth Mortgage Shopping Worksheet* (www.federalreserve.gov/pubs/mortgage/worksheet.pdf) to learn more about the mortgages you are considering.

---

* If you are considering an adjustable-rate loan, review the items listed in the *In-Depth Mortgage Shopping Worksheet* (www.federalreserve.gov/pubs/mortgage/worksheet.pdf) for more questions to ask your lender.

Why consider refinancing?

Lowering your interest rate

The interest rate on your mortgage is tied directly to how much you pay on your mortgage each month—lower rates usually mean lower payments. You may be able to get a lower rate because of changes in the market conditions or because your credit score has improved. A lower interest rate also may allow you to build equity in your home more quickly.

For example, compare the monthly payments (for principal and interest) on a 30-year fixed-rate loan of $200,000 at 5.5% and 6.0%.

Monthly payment @ 6.0%	$1,199
Monthly payment @ 5.5%	$1,136
The difference each month is	$ 63
But over a year's time, the difference adds up to	$ 756
Over 10 years, you will have saved	$7,560

Adjusting the length of your mortgage

Increase the term of your mortgage: You may want a mortgage with a longer term to reduce the amount that you pay each month. However, this will also increase the length of time you will make mortgage payments and the total amount that you end up paying toward interest.

Decrease the term of your mortgage: Shorter-term mortgages—for example, a 15-year mortgage instead of a 30-year mortgage—generally have lower interest rates. Plus, you pay off your loan sooner, further reducing your total interest costs. The trade-off is that your monthly payments usually are higher because you are paying more of the principal each month.

For example, compare the total interest costs for a fixed-rate loan of $200,000 at 6% for 30 years with a fixed-rate loan at 5.5% for 15 years.

	Monthly payment	Total interest
30-year loan @ 6.0%	$1,199	$231,640
15-year loan @ 5.5%	$1,634	$ 94,120

Changing from an adjustable-rate mortgage to a fixed-rate mortgage

If you have an adjustable-rate mortgage, or ARM, your monthly payments will change as the interest rate changes. With this kind of mortgage, your payments could increase or decrease.

You may find yourself uncomfortable with the prospect that your mortgage payments could go up. In this case, you may want to consider switching to a fixed-rate mortgage to give yourself some peace of mind by having a steady interest rate and monthly payment. You also might prefer a fixed-rate mortgage if you think interest rates will be increasing in the future.

Tip: If your monthly payment on a fixed-rate loan includes escrow amounts for taxes and insurance, your payment each month could change over time due to changes in property taxes, insurance, or community association fees.

Getting an ARM with better terms

If you currently have an ARM, will the next interest rate adjustment increase your monthly payments substantially? You may choose to refinance to get another ARM with better terms. For example, the new loan may start out at a lower interest rate.

Or the new loan may offer smaller interest rate adjustments or lower payment caps, which means that the interest rate cannot exceed a certain amount. For more details, see the *Consumer Handbook on Adjustable-Rate Mortgages* (www.federalreserve.gov/pubs/arms/arms_english.htm).

> **Tip:** If you are refinancing from one ARM to another, check the initial rate and the fully-indexed rate. Also ask about the rate adjustments you might face over the term of the loan.

Getting cash out from the equity built up in your home

Home equity is the dollar-value difference between the balance you owe on your mortgage and the value of your property. When you refinance for an amount greater than what you owe on your home, you can receive the difference in a cash payment (this is called a cash-out refinancing). You might choose to do this, for example, if you need cash to make home improvements or pay for a child's education.

Remember, though, that when you take out equity, you own less of your home. It will take time to build your equity back up. This means that if you need to sell your home, you will not put as much money in your pocket after the sale.

If you are considering a cash-out refinancing, think about other alternatives as well. You could shop for a home equity loan or home equity line of credit instead. Compare a home equity loan with a cash-out refinancing to see which is a better deal for you. See *What You Should Know about Home Equity Lines of Credit* (www.federalreserve.gov/pubs/equity/equity_english.htm).

Are you eligible to refinance?

Determining your eligibility for refinancing is similar to the approval process that you went through with your first mortgage. Your lender will consider your income and assets, credit score, other debts, the current value of the property, and the amount you want to borrow. If your credit score has improved, you may be able to get a loan at a lower rate. On the other hand, if your credit score is lower now than when you got your current mortgage, you may have to pay a higher interest rate on a new loan.

Lenders will look at the amount of the loan you request and the value of your home, determined from an appraisal. If the loan-to-value (LTV) ratio does not fall within their lending guidelines, they may not be willing to make a loan, or may offer you a loan with less-favorable terms than you already have.

If housing prices fall, your home may not be worth as much as you owe on the mortgage. Even if home prices stay the same, if you have a loan that includes negative amortization (when your monthly payment is less than the interest you owe, the unpaid interest is added to the amount you owe), you may owe more on your mortgage than you originally borrowed. If this is the case, it could be difficult for you to refinance.

What will refinancing cost?

It is not unusual to pay 3 percent to 6 percent of your outstanding principal in refinancing fees. These expenses are in addition to any prepayment penalties or other costs for paying off any mortgages you might have.

Refinancing fees vary from state to state and lender to lender. Here are some typical fees and average cost ranges you are most likely to pay when refinancing. For more information on settlement or closing costs, see the Consumer's Guide to Settlement Costs (www.federalreserve.gov/pubs/settlement/default.htm).

> Tip: You can ask for a copy of your settlement cost papers (the HUD-1 form) one day in advance of your loan closing. This will give you a chance to review the documents and verify the terms.

Application fee. This charge covers the initial costs of processing your loan request and checking your credit report. If your loan is denied, you still may have to pay this fee.
Cost range = $75 to $300

Loan origination fee. The fee charged by the lender or broker to evaluate and prepare your mortgage loan.
Cost range = 0% to 1.5% of the loan principal

Points. A point is equal to 1 percent of the amount of your mortgage loan. There are two kinds of points you might pay. The first is loan-discount points, a one-time charge paid to reduce the interest rate of your loan. Second, some lenders and brokers also charge points to earn money on the loan. The number of points you are charged can be negotiated with the lender.
Cost range = 0% to 3% of the loan principal

Appraisal fee. This fee pays for an appraisal of your home, in order to assure the lenders that the property is worth at least as much as the loan amount. Some lenders and brokers include the appraisal fee as part of the application fee. You are entitled to a copy of the appraisal, but you must ask the lender for it. If you are refinancing and you have had a recent appraisal, you can check to see if the lender will waive the requirement for a new appraisal.
Cost range = $300 to $700

Inspection fee. The lender may require a termite inspection and an analysis of the structural condition of the property by a property inspector, engineer, or consultant. Lenders may require a septic system test and a water test to make sure the well and water system will maintain an adequate supply of water for the house. Your state may require additional, specific inspections (for example, pest inspections in southern states).
Cost range = $175 to $350

Attorney review/closing fee. The lender will usually charge you for fees paid to the lawyer or company that conducts the closing for the lender.
Cost range = $500 to $1,000

Homeowner's insurance. Your lender will require that you have a homeowner's insurance policy (sometimes called hazard insurance) in effect at settlement. The policy protects against physical damage to the house by fire, wind, vandalism, and other causes covered by your policy. This policy insures that the lender's investment will be protected even if the house is destroyed. With refinancing, you may only have to show that you have a policy in effect.
Cost range = $300 to $1,000

FHA, RDS, or VA fees or PMI. These fees may be required for loans insured by federal government housing programs, such as loans insured by the Federal Housing Administration (FHA) or the Rural Development Services (RDS) and loans guaranteed by the Department of Veterans Affairs (VA), as well as conventional loans insured by private mortgage insurance (PMI). Insured loans and guarantee programs generally apply if the amount you are borrowing is more than 80% of the value of the property. Both government and private mortgage insurance cover the lender's risk that you will not make all the loan payments. **Cost ranges: FHA = 1.5% plus ½% per year; RDS = 1.75%; VA = 1.25% to 2%; PMI = 0.5% to 1.5%**

Title search and title insurance. This fee covers the cost of searching the property's records to ensure that you are the rightful owner and to check for liens. Title insurance covers the lender against errors in the results of the title search. If a problem arises, the insurance covers the lender's investment in your mortgage. **Cost range = $700 to $900**

Tip: Ask the company carrying your current title insurance policy what it would cost to reissue the policy for a new loan. This may reduce your cost.

Survey fee. Lenders require a survey, to confirm the location of buildings and improvements on the land. Some lenders require a complete (and more costly) survey to ensure that the house and other structures are legally where you say they are. You may not have to pay this fee if a survey has recently been conducted for your property. **Cost range = $150 to $400**

Prepayment penalty. Some lenders charge a fee if you pay off your existing mortgage early. Loans insured or guaranteed by the federal government generally cannot include a prepayment penalty, and some lenders, such as federal credit unions, cannot include prepayment penalties. Also some states prohibit this fee. **Cost range = one to six months' interest payments**

What is "no-cost" refinancing?

Lenders often define "no-cost" refinancing differently, so be sure to ask about the specific terms offered by each lender. Basically, there are two ways to avoid paying up-front fees.

The first is an arrangement in which the lender covers the closing costs, but charges you a higher interest rate. You will pay this higher rate for the life of the loan.

> **Tip:** Ask the lender or broker for a comparison of the up-front costs, principal, rate, and payments with and without this rate trade-off.

The second is when refinancing fees are included in ("rolled into" or "financed into") your loan—they become part of the principal you borrow. While you will not be required to pay cash up front, you will instead end up repaying these fees with interest over the life of your loan.

> **Tip:** When lenders offer a "no-cost" loan, they may include a prepayment penalty to discourage you from refinancing within the first few years of the loan. Ask the lender offering a no-cost loan to explain all the fees and penalties before you agree to these terms.

How do you calculate the break-even period?

Use the step-by-step worksheet below to give you a ballpark estimate of the time it will take to recover your refinancing costs before you benefit from a lower mortgage rate. The example assumes a $200,000, 30-year fixed-rate mortgage at 5% and a current loan at 6%. The fees for the new loan are $2,500, paid in cash at closing.

	Example	Your numbers
1. Your current monthly mortgage payment	$1,199	
2. Subtract your new monthly payment	−$1,073	
3. This equals your monthly savings	$ 126	
4. Subtract your tax rate from 1 (e.g., 1 − 0.28 = 0.72)	0.72	
5. Multiply your monthly savings (#3) by your after-tax rate (#4)	126 x 0.72	
6. This equals your after-tax savings	$ 91	
7. Total of your new loan's fees and closing costs	$2,500	
8. Divide total costs by your monthly after-tax savings (from #6)	$2,500 / 91	
9. This is the number of months it will take you to recover your refinancing costs.	27½ months	

If you plan to stay in the house until you pay off the mortgage, you may also want to look at the total interest you will pay under both the old and new loans.

You may also want to compare the equity build-up in both loans. If you have had your current loan for a while, more of your payment goes to principal, helping you build equity. If your new loan has a term that is longer than the remaining term on your existing mortgage, less of the early payments will go to principal, slowing down the equity build-up in your home.

How can you shop for your new loan?

Shopping around for a home loan will help you get the best financing deal. Shopping, comparing, and negotiating may save you thousands of dollars. Begin by getting copies of your credit reports to make sure the information in them is accurate (go to www.annualcreditreport.com for free annual copies of your report).

The *Mortgage Shopping Worksheet—A Dozen Key Questions to Ask* (on page 2) may help you. You can also use our *In-Depth Mortgage Shopping Worksheet* (at www.federalreserve.gov/pubs/ mortgage/worksheet.pdf). Take one of these worksheets with you when you talk with each lender or broker, and fill out the information provided. Don't be afraid to make lenders and brokers compete with each other for your business by letting them know that you are shopping for the best deal.

Talk to your current lender

If you plan to refinance, you may want to start with your current lender. That lender may want to keep your business, and may be willing to reduce or eliminate some of the typical refinancing fees. For example, you may be able to save on fees for the title search, surveys, and inspection. Or your lender may not charge an application fee or origination fee. This is more likely to happen if your current mortgage is only a few years old, so that paperwork relating to that loan is still current. Again, let your lender know that you are shopping around for the best deal.

Compare loans before deciding

Shop around and compare all the terms that different lenders offer—both interest rates and costs. Remember, shopping, comparing, and negotiating can save you thousands of dollars.

Lenders are required by federal law to provide a "good faith estimate" within three days of receiving your loan application. You can ask your lender for an estimate of the closing costs for the loan. The estimate should give you a detailed approximation of all costs involved in closing. Review these documents carefully and compare these costs with those for other loans. You can also ask for a copy of the HUD-1 settlement cost form one day before you are due to sign the final documents.

Tip: If you want to make sure the interest rate your lender offers you is the rate you get when you close the loan, ask about a mortgage lock-in (also called a rate lock or rate commitment). Any lock-in promise should be in writing. Make sure your lender explains any costs or obligations before you sign. See the *Consumer's Guide to Mortgage Lock-ins* (www.federalreserve.gov/pubs/lockins/default.htm).

Get information in writing

Ask for information in writing about each loan you are interested in before you pay a nonrefundable fee. It is important that you read this information and ask the lender or broker about anything you don't understand.

You may want to talk with financial advisers, housing counselors, other trusted advisers, or your attorney. To contact a local housing counseling agency, contact the U.S. Department

of Housing and Urban Development toll-free at 800-569-4287,
or visit the agency online (www.hud.gov/offices/hsg/sfh/hcc/
hccprof14.cfm) to find a center near you.

Use newspapers and the Internet to shop

Your local newspaper and the Internet are good places to start
shopping for a loan. You can usually find information on
interest rates and points offered by several lenders. Since rates
and points can change daily, you'll want to check information
sources often when shopping for a home loan.

Be careful with advertisements

Any initial information you receive about mortgages probably
will come from advertisements, mail, phone, and door-to-door
solicitations from builders, real estate brokers, mortgage brokers,
and lenders. Although this information can be helpful, keep in
mind that these are marketing materials—the ads and mailings
are designed to make the mortgage look as attractive as pos-
sible. These advertisements may play up low initial interest rates
and monthly payments, without emphasizing that those rates
and payments could increase substantially later. So get all the
facts and make sure any offers you consider meet your financial
needs.

Any ad for an ARM that shows an introductory interest rate
should also show how long the rate is in effect and the annual
percentage rate, or APR, on the loan. If the APR is much higher
than the initial rate, that is a sign that your payments may
increase a lot after the introductory period, even if market interest rates stay the same.

Tip: If there is a big difference between the initial interest rate and the APR listed in the ad, it may mean that there are high fees associated with the loan.

Choosing a mortgage may be the most important financial decision you will make. You should get all the information you need to make the right decision. Ask questions about loan features when you talk to lenders, mortgage brokers, settlement or closing agents, your attorney, and other professionals involved in the transaction—and keep asking until you get clear and complete answers.

Glossary

Adjustable-rate mortgage (ARM)

A mortgage that does not have a fixed interest rate. The rate changes during the life of the loan based on movements in an index rate, such as the rate for Treasury securities or the Cost of Funds Index. ARMs usually offer a lower initial interest rate than fixed-rate loans. The interest rate fluctuates over the life of the loan based on market conditions, but the loan agreement generally sets maximum and minimum rates. When interest rates increase, generally your loan payments increase; and when interest rates decrease, your monthly payments may decrease. For more information on ARMs, see the *Consumer Handbook on Adjustable-Rate Mortgages* (www.federalreserve.gov/pubs/arms/arms_english.htm).

Amortization

The process of fully paying off indebtedness by installments of principal and earned interest over a specific amount of time.

Annual percentage rate (APR)

The cost of credit expressed as a yearly rate. For closed-end credit, such as car loans or mortgages, the APR includes the interest rate, points, broker fees, and certain other credit charges that the borrower is required to pay. An APR, or an equivalent rate, is not used in leasing agreements.

Application fee

Fees that are charged when you apply for a loan or other credit. These fees may include charges for property appraisal and a credit report.

Appraisal fee

The charge for estimating the value of property offered as security.

Cash-out refinancing

When refinancing, taking a loan for more than you owe on your existing mortgage. Your existing mortgage is paid off and you receive an additional payment for the balance of the new loan. You might do this if you want to make home improvements or pay for a child's education. Cash-out refinancing removes some of the equity you have built up in your home.

Closing (or settlement) costs

Fees paid when you close (or settle) on a loan. These fees may include application fees; title examination, abstract of title, title insurance, and property survey fees; fees for preparing deeds, mortgages, and settlement documents; attorneys' fees; recording fees; estimated costs of taxes and insurance; and notary, appraisal, and credit report fees. Under the Real Estate Settlement Procedures Act (RESPA), the borrower receives a "good faith estimate" of closing costs within three days of application. The good faith estimate lists each expected cost as an amount or a range.

Equity

In housing markets, equity is the difference between the fair market value of the home and the outstanding balance on your mortgage plus any outstanding home equity loans. In vehicle leasing markets, equity is the positive difference between the trade-in or market value of your vehicle and the loan payoff amount.

Escrow

The holding of money or documents by a neutral third party before closing on a property. It can also be an account held by the lender (or servicer) into which a homeowner pays money for taxes and insurance.

Good faith estimate

An estimated breakdown of the costs of a mortgage loan. The Real Estate Settlement Procedures Act (RESPA) requires your mortgage lender to give you a good faith estimate of all your closing costs within 3 business days of submitting your application for a loan, whether you are purchasing or refinancing a home. The actual expenses at closing may be somewhat different from the good faith estimate.

Interest

The rate used to determine the cost of borrowing money, usually stated as a percentage and as an annual rate.

Interest rate

The price paid for borrowing money, usually stated in percentages and as an annual rate.

Loan origination fees

Fees charged by the lender for processing a loan; often expressed as a percentage of the loan amount.

Lock-in agreement

A written agreement guaranteeing a homebuyer a specific interest rate on a home loan provided that the loan is closed within a certain period, such as 60 or 90 days. Often the agreement also specifies the number of points to be paid at closing.

Mortgage

A contract, signed by a borrower when a home loan is made, that gives the lender the right to take possession of the property if the borrower fails to pay off, or defaults on, the loan.

Negative amortization

Occurs when the monthly payments in an adjustable-rate mortgage loan do not cover all the interest owed. The interest that is not paid in the monthly payment is added to the loan balance. This means that even after making many payments, you could owe more than you did at the beginning of the loan. Negative amortization can occur when an ARM has a payment cap that results in monthly payments that are not high enough to cover the interest due or when the minimum payments are set at an amount lower than the amount you owe in interest.

Payment cap

A limit on the amount that your monthly mortgage payment on a loan may change, usually a percentage of the loan. The limit can be applied each time the payment changes or during the life of the mortgage. Payment caps may lead to negative amortization because they do not limit the amount of interest the lender is earning.

Points (also called discount points)

One point is equal to 1 percent of the principal amount of a mortgage loan. For example, if a mortgage is $200,000, one point equals $2,000. Lenders frequently charge points in both fixed-rate and adjustable-rate mortgages to cover loan origination costs or to provide additional compensation to the lender or broker. Points are paid usually on the loan closing date and may be paid by the borrower or the home seller, or split between the two parties. In some cases, the money needed to pay points can be borrowed, but doing so will increase the loan amount and the total costs. Discount points (sometimes called discount fees) are points that the borrower voluntarily chooses to pay in return for a lower interest rate.

Prepayment penalty

Extra fees that may be due if you pay off your loan early by refinancing the loan or by selling the home. The penalty is usually limited to the first 3 to 5 years of the loan's term. If your loan includes a prepayment penalty, make sure you understand the cost. Compare the length of the prepayment penalty period with the first adjustment period of the ARM to see if refinancing is cost-effective before the loan first adjusts. Some loans may have a prepayment penalty even if you make a partial prepayment. Ask the lender for a loan without a prepayment penalty and the cost of that loan.

Principal

The amount of money borrowed or the amount still owed on a loan.

Refinancing

The process of paying off an existing mortgage by taking out a new mortgage.

Term

The period from the time that a loan is made until it is fully paid.

Where to go for help

Help

For additional information or to file a complaint about a bank, savings and loan, credit union, or other financial institution, contact one of the following federal agencies, depending on the type of institution.

State-chartered bank members of the Federal Reserve System
Federal Reserve Consumer Help
PO Box 1200
Minneapolis, MN 55480
888-851-1920 (toll free)
877-766-8533 (TTY) (toll free)
877-888-2520 (fax) (toll free)
e-mail: ConsumerHelp@FederalReserve.gov
www.FederalReserveConsumerHelp.gov

National banks[1] and national-bank-owned mortgage companies
Office of the Comptroller of the Currency (OCC)
Customer Assistance Group
1301 McKinney Street, Suite 3450
Houston, TX 77010
800-613-6743 (toll free)
713-336-4301 (fax)
e-mail: customer.assistance@occ.treas.gov
www.occ.treas.gov
www.helpwithmybank.gov

Federally chartered credit unions[2]
National Credit Union Administration (NCUA)
Office of Public and Congressional Affairs
1775 Duke Street
Alexandria, VA 22314
800-755-1030 (toll free)
703-518-6409 (fax)
e-mail: consumerassistance@ncua.gov
www.ncua.gov/ConsumerInformation/index.htm

---

[1] Banks with "National" in their name or "N.A." after the name.
[2] Credit unions with "Federal" in their name.

For state-chartered credit unions, contact the regulatory agency in the state in which the credit union is chartered.
www.ncua.gov/consumerinformation/consumer%20complaints/statechartered.htm

Federally insured state-chartered banks that are not members of the Federal Reserve System
Federal Deposit Insurance Corporation (FDIC)
Consumer Response Center
2345 Grand Blvd., Suite 100
Kansas City, MO 64108
877-ASK-FDIC (877-275-3342) (toll free)
e-mail: consumeralerts@fdic.gov
www.fdic.gov/consumers/consumer/ccc/index.html

Savings and loan associations[3]
Office of Thrift Supervision (OTS)
Consumer Affairs
1700 G Street, NW
Washington, DC 20552
800-842-6929 (toll free)
800-877-8339 (TTY) (toll free)
www.ots.treas.gov

Mortgage companies and other lenders
Federal Trade Commission (FTC)
Consumer Response Center
600 Pennsylvania Avenue, NW
Washington, DC 20580
202-326-3758 or (877) FTC-HELP
866-FTC-HELP (877-382-4357) (toll free)
www.ftc.gov

---

[3] Federally chartered and some state-chartered associations.

More resources and ordering information

Other mortgage publications available from the Federal Reserve include:

A Consumer's Guide to Mortgage Lock-Ins
www.federalreserve.gov/pubs/lockins/default.htm

A Consumer's Guide to Mortgage Settlement Costs
www.federalreserve.gov/pubs/settlement/default.htm

Consumer Handbook on Adjustable-Rate Mortgages (ARM)
www.federalreserve.gov/pubs/arms/arms_english.htm

Home Mortgages: Understanding the Process and Your Right to Fair Lending
www.federalreserve.gov/pubs/mortgage/morbro.htm

Interest-Only Mortgage Payments and Payment-Option ARMs—Are They for You?
www.federalreserve.gov/pubs/mortgage_interestonly/

Looking for the Best Mortgage: Shop, Compare, Negotiate
www.federalreserve.gov/pubs/mortgage/mortb_1.htm

Putting Your Home on the Loan Line Is Risky Business
www.federalreserve.gov/pubs/riskyhomeloans/default.htm

What You Should Know about Home Equity Lines of Credit
www.federalreserve.gov/pubs/equity/equity_english.htm

For more information on mortgage and other financial topics, including interactive calculators, visit www.federalreserve.gov/consumerinfo.

The Federal Reserve Board and the Office of Thrift Supervision prepared this information on refinancing your mortgage in response to a request from the House Committee on Banking, Finance, and Urban Affairs and in consultation with the following organizations:

Community Bankers Association
Consumer Federation of America
Credit Union National Administration
Fannie Mae
Federal Deposit Insurance Corporation
Federal Reserve Bank of Philadelphia
Federal Trade Commission
Freddie Mac
Mortgage Bankers Association
Mortgage Insurance Companies of America
National Association of Home Builders
National Association of Realtors
National Credit Union Administration
Office of the Comptroller of the Currency
U.S. Department of Housing and Urban Development